HEART DISEASE

HEART DISEASE

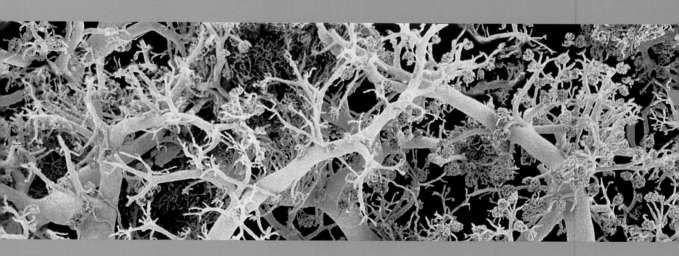

Johannah Haney

BENCHMARK BOOKS

MARSHALL CAVENDISH
NEW YORK

With thanks to Renato N. Mascardo, M.D., FACE, FACP, Assistant Clinical Professor of Medicine, Division of Endocrinology & Metabolism, University of Connecticut School of Medicine, for his expert review of the manuscript

Benchmark Books
Marshall Cavendish
99 White Plains Road
Tarrytown, New York 10591-9001
www.marshallcavendish.com

Library of Congress Cataloging-in-Publication Data

Haney, Johannah.
   Heart disease / by Johannah Haney.
      p. cm. — (Health alert)
   Includes bibliographical references and index.
   ISBN 0-7614-1801-6
   1. Heart—Diseases—Juvenile literature. I. Title. II. Series: Health alert (Benchmark Books).

   RC673.H36 2005
   616.1'2—dc22

                         2004005974

Front cover: The human heart.
Title page: Blood vessels

Photo research by Regina Flanagan
Front Cover: Mehau Kulyk / Photo Researchers, Inc.

The photographs in this book are used by permission and through the courtesy of: *Photo Researchers, Inc:* Francis Leroy, 13; John Bavosi, 14, 28; Susumu Nishinaga, 15; SPL, 17, 27, 38, 39; Mark Thomas, 18; CC Studio, 20; St. Bartholomew's Hospital, London, 23; Medical Art Service, 16; Peter Gardiner, 25; Gusto, 29; Du Cane Medical Imaging LTD, 33; Alexander Tsiaras, 35; G. Bernard, 37; Antonia Reeve, 41; Hank Morgan, 44; James King-Holmes, 45; Larry Mulvehill, 55. *Corbis:* 26; Digital Art, 11; Hulton-Deutsch Collection, 40; Bettmann, 43; Ron Slenzak, 48; Ken Redding, 49; Ariel Skelley, 51; Bennett Dean / Eye Ubiquitous, 52; Dex Images, 53; William Whitehurst, 54. *Picture Quest:* Mitch Hrdlicka / Photodisc, 47.

Printed in China

6 5 4 3 2 1

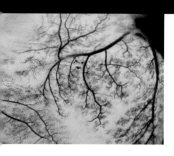

CONTENTS

1

WHAT IS IT LIKE TO HAVE HEART DISEASE?

There are many different types of heart disease. Some types are present at birth. Other types develop as a person gets older. Heart disease is very serious, but there are many different things that doctors can do to treat it. Certain types of heart disease can be prevented by eating a balanced diet, exercising regularly, not smoking, and seeing a doctor for regular check-ups.

JOSIE

Before babies are born, they grow and develop inside their mothers. As they grow, they develop organs and body parts such as bones, skin, lungs, a brain, blood vessels, and a heart. An unborn baby's heart and blood vessels are not completely formed. Until the baby is born, there is a small hole that allows the blood to skip going to the lungs. When a baby is born and takes its first breath, this hole is supposed to close up and blood can then flow from the heart to the lungs through blood vessels. But for many babies who are born **prematurely** (early), and even for some who are born on time, this hole does not close as it should, causing health problems. If the hole is not closed, a baby's heart and lungs will not function properly. Breathing problems can develop and his or her heart may get infected, causing more problems. A baby with this problem also might not be able to eat enough, and as a result, would not grow well.

Josie is a little girl who was affected by this form of heart disease. She was born almost three months prematurely and the hole in her heart had not closed. Fortunately, doctors quickly discovered the problem and performed surgery to fix the hole. After the surgery, the bloodflow through Josie's heart, and between her heart and lungs, was normal.

Because her heart was repaired, Josie can grow and develop like other children. She still has to visit special doctors who check on her heart, but today she is a healthy and happy little girl.

ASPEN

Aspen was a forty-year-old woman with a busy life. She worked many hours at a very busy job and often felt very anxious or worried. Aspen did not eat **nutritious** foods, which are rich in vitamins and minerals, but instead preferred fast food and junk food. She also did not take time to exercise regularly.

One day at work she felt pain in her chest. Within minutes the pain became worse, until she felt like there was an elephant sitting on her chest. She was also having stomach pains and felt like she was going to vomit. She knew something was wrong, so she asked her coworker to take her to the hospital. On the way to the hospital, Aspen started to feel like she was going to **faint.** She had a hard time catching her breath and she began to sweat a lot.

Once Aspen arrived at the hospital, doctors began to run tests to see if she was having a heart attack. They did an **electrocardiogram** (EKG) test. This test involved taping electrodes to her chest, arms, and legs. The electrodes are thin wires connected to a machine which measured the activity of her heart. Doctors also took a sample of her blood and tested it for a chemical that is present when a person is having a heart attack. When the test results came back, the doctors told Aspen that she was indeed having a heart attack.

Aspen's problem was that her heart was not getting enough oxygen. Normally, the heart gets its oxygen from the bloodstream, just as every other part of the body does. It has its own blood vessels, which bring blood to it and supply the oxygen and nutrients the heart needs. But the vessels going to Aspen's heart were blocked with a substance called **plaque** (not the same thing as the stuff that can build up on teeth).

Because blood could not get to Aspen's heart, parts of it were dying and it could not function properly. Aspen needed medicine and surgery. Doctors decided to perform a procedure called **angioplasty.** By using this procedure, doctors were able to flatten the plaque that was blocking the artery. Soon Aspen's blood was flowing properly.

Aspen had to stay at the hospital for a few days after the surgery. Once she went home, she began to change her habits so that she could become healthier. She worked less and tried to reduce the **stress** in her life. Aspen stopped eating a lot of junk food and began to eat more healthful meals. She also began to exercise. She took long walks, jogged, and swam.

Today, Aspen is much healthier. She still visits her doctor for check-ups, she eats right, and she exercises. She has learned from her experience and does not want heart disease to get in the way of living a long, fulfilling life.

2

WHAT IS HEART DISEASE?

The human heart is an amazing organ. It has one of the most important jobs—to keep blood flowing throughout the body. Any condition or injury that keeps the heart from operating properly is called heart disease. In order to see how heart disease affects a person, you must first understand how a human heart functions.

ALL ABOUT THE HEART

A human heart is located inside the chest, a little to the left of the center of the chest. It is about the size of a fist and is protected by the ribcage and breastbone. The heart is also surrounded and held in place by a special covering called the **pericardium**. The heart is actually a muscle, and is made up of a special type of muscle tissue called the **myocardium** (*myo* means "muscle" and *cardium* refers to "heart.") Unlike most other muscles in your body, the myocardium works on its own. For example, in order for the muscles in your leg to work, the brain must send a direct signal to them, which makes them move. But the heart has its own command center, called the **sinoatrial node,** which sends an electrical impulse to keep the heart beating. When the heart works, it squeezes tight then relaxes, then squeezes again and relaxes, and so on. Imagine if you made a tight fist with your hand and then let it relax, then tightened it again, and relaxed it, and did this over and over. That would be something like a beating heart.

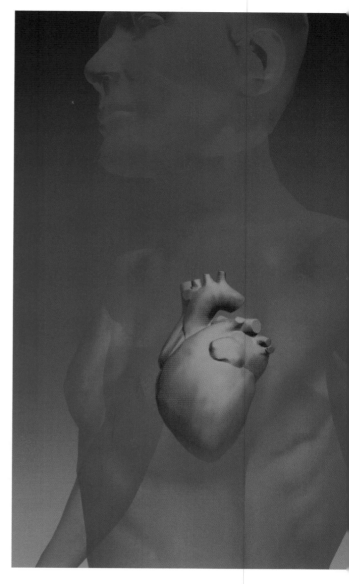

This computer-generated image shows the location of the heart in a healthy adult.

Although the heart will beat on its own, the brain sends signals to it that will make it go faster or slower as needed by the body. For example, exercising makes the heart beat faster because the muscles need more blood and oxygen than when they are resting.

The heart's job is to keep blood moving to all parts of the body. It does this by acting like a pump. Several times a minute the heart fills with blood and squeezes tight, forcing the blood out again. The blood moves through vessels that go to all parts of the body.

The inside of the heart is much more than just a hollow space. It has four separate areas, or **chambers**, that fill with blood. There is one upper chamber on the left side of the heart, and one on the right side. Each of these upper chambers is called an **atrium** (plural of atrium is atria.) The lower chambers of the heart are called **ventricles**. A strong wall of muscle called the **septum** divides the heart into right and left sides. It keeps blood from the left atrium and right atrium separate. It also keeps blood in the two ventricles separate.

There are four **valves** in the heart. Valves are one-way openings through which blood can flow forward. They prevent blood from flowing backward. There is a valve between each atrium and the ventricle below it. When the heart beats, the

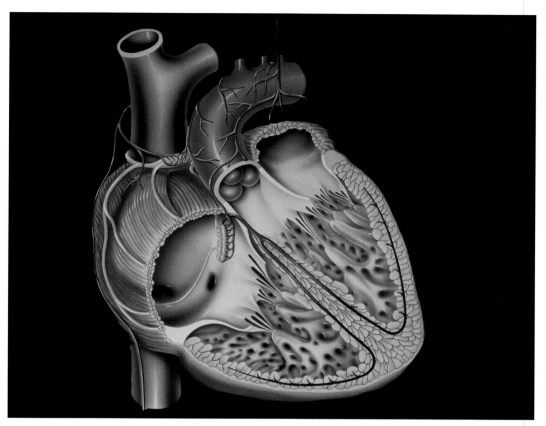

An illustration of a heart reveals the heart's four chambers.

valves open, allowing blood to move from the atria into the ventricles. The valves then close so blood does not move back into the atria. In the meantime, more blood has filled the atria. At the next heartbeat, the valves open once again, and blood from the atria moves into the ventricles. At the same time, blood that was in the ventricles gets squeezed out of

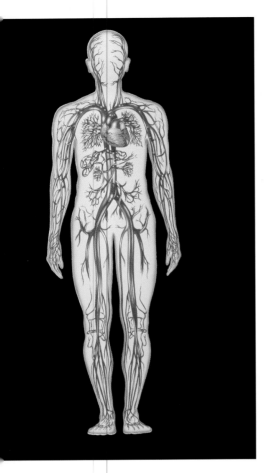

The circulatory system is a complex network of blood vessels of different sizes. The vessels carry blood to and from organs and other parts of the body.

the heart and into blood vessels. There are valves in each of the two large vessels that carry blood away from the heart. They keep blood from flowing back into the ventricles.

The pattern of blood flowing through the heart and into vessels is repeated many times a minute, for as long as a person is alive.

Blood Vessels

The heart's job is to continually pump blood. The blood delivers nutrients and oxygen, but also takes away waste material from cells. Blood travels through the body through blood vessels. Blood vessels are hollow tubes of different sizes. Some carry blood away from the heart. These are called arteries. Blood from the left ventricle first travels through the **aorta**, the largest artery in the human body. It is about as big around as a person's thumb. The force at which the blood moves through the aorta is so strong that it could send water shooting six feet into the air. The aorta branches off into many smaller arteries. They carry blood toward the head, arms, chest, **abdomen**, and legs. These arteries branch into even smaller arteries called arterioles. Arterioles are about the width of a piece of thread. Arterioles branch off into capillaries, which are the smallest type of blood vessel. A human body has about ten billion capillaries. Capillaries are too small to see without a microscope, and are about the width of one single red blood cell. The walls of capillaries are very thin, which allows nutrients and oxygen from the blood to cross the capillary

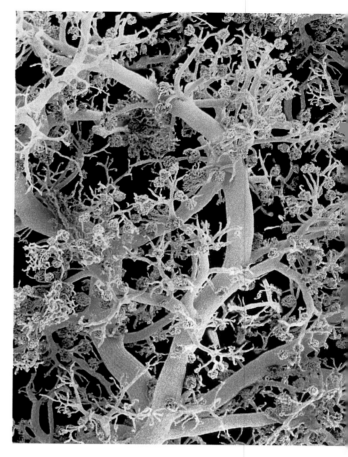

Large blood vessels branch off into smaller ones. This electron micrograph (enlarged picture) shows the delicate system of blood vessels found in the kidneys.

walls and get into cells. In addition, waste from cells enters the blood through the capillaries.

After the nutrients and oxygen in blood have been supplied to the cells in the body, and waste from cells picked up, the blood returns to the heart. Vessels that return blood to the heart are called **veins.** From the capillaries, blood first enters

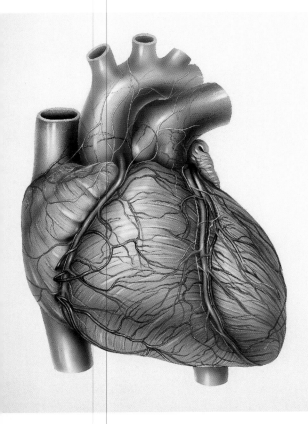

The upper and lower vena cava are shown in blue on the left side of this illustration. The aorta is the large red blood vessel at the top of the heart. The pulmonary arteries are shown in purple, below the aorta.

tiny veins called **venules.** Venules join together into larger veins. Some of these larger veins have valves that open and shut so that blood can only flow in one direction—toward the heart.

As blood gets closer to the heart, all veins feed into two large veins: the upper vena cava and the lower vena cava. The upper vena cava carries blood returning from the head, the arms, and chest. The lower vena cava carries blood returning from the abdomen and legs. Both the upper vena cava and the lower vena cava bring blood into the right atrium of the heart. But the right atrium is not very large. It can only hold a small amount of blood at a time. Where does all that blood coming back from the veins go?

Each time the heart muscle squeezes, it pushes blood from the right atrium into the right ventricle. The right ventricle then pumps blood into the pulmonary arteries, which carry blood away from the heart again. These arteries lead to the lungs. In the lungs, blood is given a fresh supply of oxygen. This oxygen-rich blood then travels through pulmonary veins which lead to the heart's left atrium. The blood then moves from the left atrium into the left ventricle.

As described earlier, blood in the left ventricle leaves the heart and enters the aorta. The aorta carries the blood to arteries, arterioles, capillaries, and so on. The process repeats over and over. Blood is constantly entering the atria and being pumped out by ventricles.

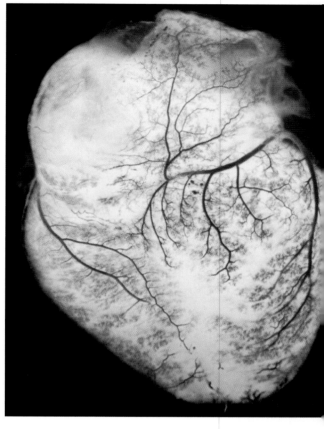

Delicate webs of coronary arteries and veins supply the heart muscle with blood. Without oxygen-rich blood from the arteries, the heart muscle will weaken or die.

Some of the blood in the aorta goes into the coronary arteries. These small arteries supply the heart muscle itself with oxygen-rich blood. If the coronary arteries become blocked, heart muscle cannot get oxygen, and will begin to die. This problem is the main reason why people have heart attacks.

The Amazing Heart

The heart beats several times each minute. The number of times the heart beats each minute is called the heart rate or pulse rate. The average adult heart rate is between 60 and 90 beats per minute. Heartbeats can be heard in a person's chest. Blood that is pulsing through arteries at the same rhythm can be felt in the wrist, thumb, and neck. The average heart beats 100,000 times in a single day, pumping about 2,000 gallons of blood.

If you are	your heart has beaten about...
8 years old	292 million times
9 years old	328.5 million times
10 years old	365 million times
11 years old	401.5 million times
12 years old	438 million times
13 years old	474.5 million times

You can check your (or someone else's) pulse rate by counting the number of pulses per minute.

CONGENITAL HEART DEFECTS

The word congenital means existing at birth. Congenital heart defects are problems with the heart that are present from the time a baby is born. Each year in the United States, over 25,000 babies are born with congenital heart defects. There are many different types of congenital heart defects. Most are due to the improper formation of the heart during its development in the unborn baby. For example, a valve might not close properly because it is the wrong shape, or one of the heart's chambers might not become completely separate from another.

Patent Ductus Arteriosus (PDA)

An example of a congenital heart defect is patent ductus arteriosus, or PDA. Before a baby is born, blood does not travel through the pulmonary arteries to the lungs. Instead, blood travels through a blood vessel called the ductus arteriosus, which connects the pulmonary artery to the aorta. The ductus arteriosus sends blood to the aorta instead of to the lungs. (The lungs are not being used by an unborn baby, so blood does not need to go there.) But, when a baby is born and takes his or her first breath, the ductus arteriosus is supposed to close. Once it closes, blood flows into the lungs to get oxygen.

In babies with PDA, the ductus arteriosus does not close as it should. Infants with PDA may have a hard time breathing. PDA can also lead to poor growth. If a baby with PDA was born prematurely, then medications can help speed the natural changes that need to happen in the heart and vessels. However, these medications will not work in babies who were not born too early. These babies will need surgery to correct the problem.

Septal Defects

When an unborn baby's heart is forming, the septum between the two atria has a hole in it, which allows blood to leak from

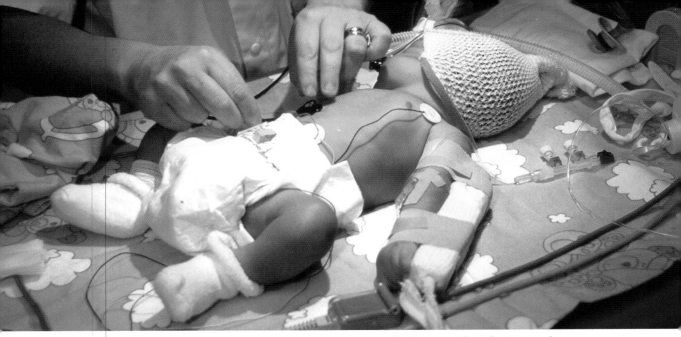

Small electrodes are attached to this premature baby's chest so that doctors and nurses can monitor his heart rate.

the right side into the left side of the heart. This is another way that blood (in an unborn baby) is kept from going to the lungs before they can be used for breathing air. The hole allows blood that would have gone to the lungs to get pumped into the aorta instead.

The hole normally closes shortly after a baby is born. But in some babies, it stays open. After a baby with this problem is born, his or her heart has to work harder. This extra work can lead to the heart becoming tired and weak. The heart can also grow too big because of the extra work it must do.

An AV septal defect (AV stands for atrium and ventricle) occurs when there is a hole in the septum where the upper and lower chambers of the heart meet. In an AV septal defect, blood is flowing freely among all chambers of the heart. AV septal defects are serious, and if left untreated can lead to too much pressure in the lungs or heart failure.

If a child has a septal defect, it is usually repaired with surgery before the age of five. Surgery to correct a hole in the septum between atria often involves patching the hole with synthetic (manmade) material, or with pieces of the person's pericardium. Doctors do the surgery through a thin tube inserted into the chest, rather than performing open-heart surgery. When doctors are fixing an AV septal defect, surgery is required much sooner, usually before an infant is nine months old.

Coarctation of the Aorta

The word coarctation means "narrow." Coarctation of the aorta means that a section of the aorta is too narrow for the blood to pass easily. This means that less blood can flow through it. If the problem is not fixed, the heart may have to work too hard to pump blood. Blood pressure can also be too low. (Blood pressure is the force at which the blood is moving through the arteries when the heart pumps blood into them.)

Coarctation of the aorta is treated with surgery. Doctors remove the narrow portion of the aorta and sew the two normal-sized ends together. Another way doctors can fix coarctation of the aorta is by inserting a balloon into the narrow portion and inflating it enough to widen the passageway. This surgery usually requires a patient to be in the hospital for a few days. If this surgery is performed before a child is ten years old, the chance of having normal heart function and a normal life are good.

Tetralogy of Fallot

Tetralogy of Fallot is really a combination of four heart defects. There is a hole in the septum between the right and left ventricles; a blockage between the right ventricle and the lungs; an enlarged right ventricle; and an improperly placed aorta. Infants with Tetralogy of Fallot often look like their skin is blue. This is because the defects prevent blood from getting enough oxygen. This blood looks blue through the skin (although it is dark red in color).

Babies who are born with this condition need surgery. Sometimes two surgeries are needed. The first surgery improves blood flow to the lungs and decreases the blue color of the skin. The second surgery clears the blockage between the ventricle and lung and patches the hole in the septum. Until these can be performed, parents and health care providers can do things to make life a little easier for children with the Tetralogy of Fallot. For example, feeding a child more slowly can reduce the amount of energy used for eating and digesting. This can help the level of oxygen in the blood stay higher. If a child has blue lips or fingernails from lack of oxygen in the blood, lying in a knee-to-chest position can help. Giving the child oxygen through a breathing mask also helps.

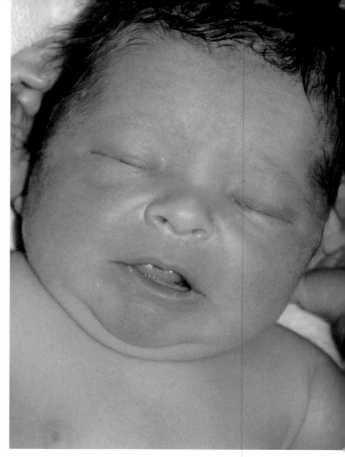

The blue color of this baby's skin comes from oxygen-poor blood being pumped throughout his body. Surgery can fix the congenital heart defect that is causing this condition.

Transposition of the Great Arteries (TGA)

The word transpose means to reverse. In TGA, the aorta and pulmonary arteries are switched. The aorta receives blood that is not oxygen-rich and delivers it to the rest of the body, while pulmonary arteries receive oxygen-rich blood, but deliver it right back to the lungs. As a result, not enough oxygen is in the blood for cells to use.

Doctors must treat transposition of the great arteries through surgery. During surgery, the aorta is cut and sewn in the proper place. The pulmonary arteries are also cut and sewn into the right place. In some cases doctors cannot perform surgery right away because a baby is too small or cannot survive a long surgery. In these cases, doctors do a shorter procedure to put a band around the pulmonary artery. This helps keep too much pressure from building in the lungs, and allows the baby more time to grow until the full surgery can be performed.

OTHER TYPES OF HEART DISEASE

According to the Centers for Disease Control, 61 million Americans live with heart disease. Most of them were born with normal hearts but developed some type of heart disease during their lives. One of the most common types of heart disease is a heart attack. Other types include **hypertension**, arrhythmia, and congestive heart failure.

Heart Attack

A heart attack takes place when part of the heart muscle does not get enough blood from the coronary arteries. In most cases this is because the coronary arteries become blocked by a substance called plaque. Plaque in coronary arteries is from a buildup of fatlike material and cells that collect on the inside of the blood vessel. The plaque itself can block the artery, or it can cause blood clots to form. The blood clots may also block the bloodflow in the artery. Blood in the coronary arteries supplies fresh oxygen to the myocardium.

When heart muscle does not get enough oxygen, it begins to die. When that happens, the heart cannot pump blood well and that can cause a person to die. The medical term for a heart attack is myocardial infarction, or MI.

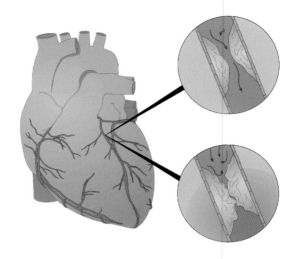

Heart attacks can be painful. People who have had heart attacks describe the pain as a great pressure, as if something were sitting on their chest. Some people also

The yellow substance in the illustration is fatty plaque that is blocking coronary arteries. A healthful diet and regular exercise can often help to decrease plaque buildup.

experience pain in the neck and shoulder, and the pain can travel down the arm. Women may feel breathless or feel sick, but without pain. Many do feel pain in the chest, and also in the jaw, stomach, arms, and back. But this pain may not be as intense (strong) in some women.

When a person thinks he or she is having a heart attack, quick medical treatment can mean the difference between living and dying. Someone should call 911 to get medical help as quickly as possible. The person having a heart attack needs to go to the emergency room right away. The first thing a doctor will do is decide whether the person really is having a

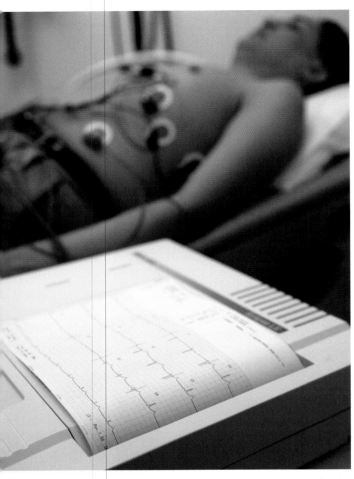

Medical professionals can "read" the squiggly lines printed on the paper coming from the EKG machine. These lines represent a patients heart activity.

heart attack. One test used to decide this is an electro-cardiogram (EKG). To do this, medical staff attach electrodes to certain points on the chest, arms, and legs. These sensitive electrodes will record the heart's electrical activity. Doctors can tell whether a person is having a heart attack, or has recently had one, based on the EKG results. Blood tests can also show whether a person is having a heart attack. During a heart attack, special chemicals are released into the bloodstream. Medical staff can test to see if any of those chemicals are in the blood.

Once doctors determine that a person is having a heart attack, the patient will usually be given medication to prevent any more artery blockage. Another medication a person experiencing a heart attack might receive is nitroglycerin, which is sprayed under the tongue of the patient. Nitroglycerin relaxes blood vessels so blood can flow more easily and the heart can stop working so hard. Medications called clot busters can also be given to help dissolve any blood clot that might be blocking the blood vessel. A doctor will decide which medications will work best for each patient.

Sometimes a person suffering from a heart attack will need surgery to open a blocked coronary artery. One surgical procedure that does this is angioplasty. Doctors insert a small balloon into the artery and inflate it. This presses plaque against the artery wall, leaving more room for

The balloon device used during angioplasty is very small and very delicate.

blood to flow through it after the balloon is removed. After angioplasty, doctors sometimes insert a **stent** into the artery. A stent is a wire mesh tube that holds the artery open.

Another surgical procedure for heart attack patients is coronary bypass surgery. Doctors take a vein from somewhere else in the body and use it to replace the blocked coronary artery. The vein is often taken from the leg or chest. Doctors connect the vein to the coronary artery on both sides of the blocked area. Blood then flows through the piece of vein, going around—or bypassing—the blocked area. It is common for a person to have three or four coronary arteries fixed this way, all during a single surgery.

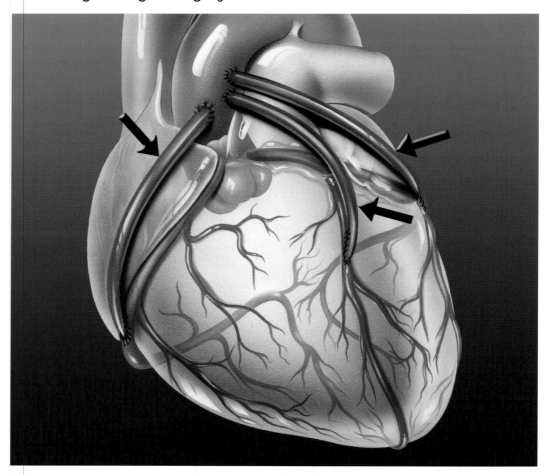

Veins taken from other parts of the body (indicated by the arrows) were used to bypass blocked coronary arteries.

High Blood Pressure

High blood pressure occurs when the force of blood through the arteries is too strong. It is also known as hypertension. The cause of hypertension is unknown in many cases, though plaque buildup in many of the body's arteries is one cause. Blood pressure can be measured at a doctor's office or at home with a device called a **sphygmomanometer**. Part of the device is a cloth band that is placed around the upper arm. Attached to the band is a pump, which inflates the band with air. This tightens the band and stops the flow of blood in the arteries of the arm for just a moment. The air is let out gradually, and the pressure of blood in the artery is measured as the blood begins to flow again. A doctor or nurse can tell when the blood is flowing again by listening for it pulsing, with the aid of a stethoscope (an instrument used to hear sounds inside the body).

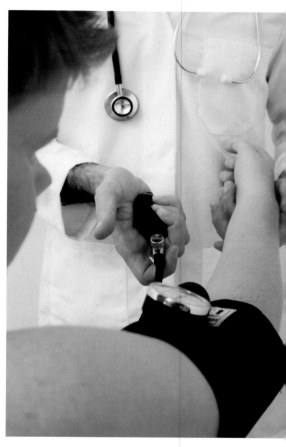

Doctors routinely measure the blood pressure of patients of all ages. Here, a doctor takes blood pressure using a sphygmomanometer.

A blood pressure reading has two numbers. The first is called the systolic pressure. The systolic pressure measures the pressure in the arm's artery just after the heart squeezes and forces blood into the arteries. The second number is the diastolic pressure. The diastolic pressure is the pressure of blood when the heart is at rest for a moment, between beats. A complete blood pressure reading is given as the systolic reading over the diastolic reading. For example, if the systolic reading is 120 and the diastolic reading is 80, a doctor would say that the blood pressure result is "120 over 80." A healthy blood pressure reading is under 120 systolic pressure, and under 80 diastolic pressure. A systolic reading between 120 and 139, and a diastolic reading between 80 and 89 are considered prehypertension. Pre means "before," so prehypertension means that blood pressure is not normal, but it is not yet high enough to be called hypertension. Readings over 140 systolic and 90 diastolic indicate hypertension, which is dangerous.

When a person has high blood pressure, the heart must work harder to force blood along, and arteries are under more pressure than is healthy. Hypertension can increase a person's risk for other heart problems, such as a heart attack and congestive heart failure. Often a person with hypertension does not experience any symptoms. This is one of the reasons it is so dangerous. A person could have hypertension for years and never know it.

But once it is diagnosed, it can be treated through medication, exercise, and diet.

Arrhythmia

Just like keeping time in music, the heart beats to a rhythm. The average adult heart beats about 60 to 90 times per minute, depending on the size and age of a person. The number of beats goes up while a person exercizes, and for a while afterward.

An arrhythmia occurs when the heart rate is abnormal. **Tachycardia** is when the heart beats too quickly. In some instances, tachycardia can cause the heart to become too large. This is because the heart is working harder and the muscle grows (just like running a lot causes leg muscles to increase in size). Certain kinds

Stroke

Technically, strokes are not a type of heart disease. But a stroke can be caused by different forms of heart disease. In the United States, about 700,000 people suffer from a stroke every year.

A stroke happens when the brain does not get enough oxygen. Arteries leading to the brain can become blocked by a blood clot. When blood to the brain is blocked, not enough oxygen reaches parts of the brain and the cells in that part of the brain begin to die. Each part of the brain is responsible for controlling function in a specific part of the body. When part of the brain dies from lack of oxygen, the part of the body that it controls is affected. For example, if a stroke affects the part of the brain that controls speech, the person who had a stroke might have difficulty speaking. Strokes can also affect vision, motion, memory, or speech. However, stroke survivors can work with physical or **rehabilitation** therapists to try to repair some of the damage.

of tachycardia can be very dangerous and can quickly cause a person to lose consciousness or die. **Bradycardia** is when the heart beats too slowly. A person with bradycardia might feel lightheaded, dizzy, or faint.

Treatment for an arrhythmia depends on what kind and how severe (serious) it is. For the most mild cases, lifestyle changes like quitting smoking, avoiding caffeine, managing stress, and avoiding certain medications can be enough to stay healthy. More serious arrhythmias require medication and, sometimes, surgery. Medication is used to control the rhythm of the heart so that it remains close to normal. People taking medication for arrhythmias need to check their pulse regularly. There are different surgical procedures for the different arrhythmias. Bradycardia is sometimes treated by inserting a **pacemaker** near the heart. This is a small device that detects a slow heart rate and delivers an electrical impulse to stimulate the heart to beat at a normal rate. Tachycardia is sometimes treated with a surgical procedure in which an implanted cardioverter defibrillator (ICD) is placed in the chest. An ICD corrects a fast heart rate. For sudden cases of very irregular heart beat rhythm, a person must have immediate medical attention. A very strong electrical shock can be given, using a portable defibrillator machine. This can set the heart's own rhythm back to normal.

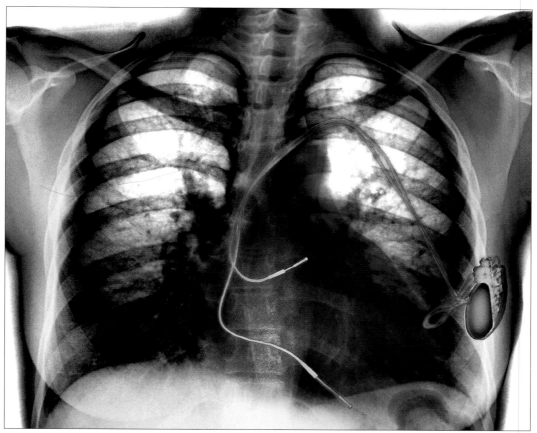

A colored X ray shows an implanted pacemaker (right) and the wires (center) that lead to the heart. These wires deliver electrical impulses to regulate heartbeat.

Congestive Heart Failure

Congestive heart failure affects five million Americans. When a person has congestive heart failure, the heart does not pump as well as it should. This can be due to weak heart muscle or leaky valves. This can happen on the left side of the heart, on the right side of the heart, or on both sides. When it affects the left side of the heart, blood coming back from the lungs collects in the heart's left side. The blood may then leak backward into the blood vessels of the lungs. This creates breathing problems and causes fluid to build up in the lungs. When congestive heart failure affects the right side of the heart, blood returning to the heart collects in its right side, and backs up in the veins. As blood collects in the veins, it causes swelling in the body, especially in the abdomen and legs.

Congestive heart failure usually does not occur by itself. The heart is often affected by other kinds of heart disease as well. This might include a previous heart attack, hypertension, an infection, congenital heart disease, or an arrhythmia. Any of these conditions can make the heart a weaker pump. If left untreated, they can lead to congestive heart failure.

To treat congestive heart failure, doctors must first treat the heart disease that led to it. Sometimes, especially when hypertension or blocked arteries are to blame, the condition can be reversed. Other times, the damage to the heart is permanent.

Doctors and scientists have found some interesting ways to help patients whose hearts are damaged. One of these is valve replacement surgery. This surgery involves removing a valve in the heart that is not working properly. A new valve is inserted in its place. The new valve can be from a donor heart, or an artificial valve that is manmade.

Another amazing heart surgery is a heart transplant. In a heart transplant, doctors remove the diseased or damaged heart and replace it with the healthy heart of someone who has recently died and donated his or her heart. About 100,000 people need a heart transplant each year, but there are not enough donor hearts. Patients who have received transplants must continue to take medications that prevent their bodies from rejecting the new heart. They must also see their doctors regularly for the rest of their lives.

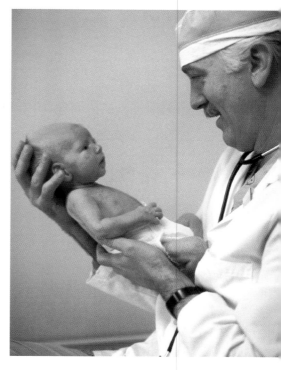

Thanks to new technologies and many years of research, physicians can perform successful heart transplants on very young babies.

Despite the seriousness of heart disease, it does not mean that a person's life is over. If symptoms are caught early enough, and proper treatment is followed, it is very likely that people with heart disease can go on to lead normal lives. It helps to know how the heart works, learn what can go wrong, and be aware of what factors can increase a person's chance of getting heart disease.

3

THE HISTORY OF HEART DISEASE

For thousands of years, humans have known about the importance of the heart. In ancient Egypt, doctors understood a little about the heart. They believed it was the central meeting point for vessels. These vessels carried all of the different body fluids throughout the body. This included blood, tears, and urine. While these early doctors were wrong about tears and urine, they were right to associate the heart with blood. Ancient Egyptians used herbal remedies like aloe vera, juniper, mustard, and onion to soothe chest pain and heart problems.

Over the years, as technology improved, scientists and doctors learned more about the human heart. Many scientists **dissected** the hearts of people who had died from heart problems. By examining the heart's structure, they were able to develop theories of how the heart worked, what went wrong,

Artwork from medieval times displays a man suffering from a heart attack or a stroke. Unfortunately, scientists and physicians at that time did not know how to successfully treat or prevent heart attacks and other heart conditions.

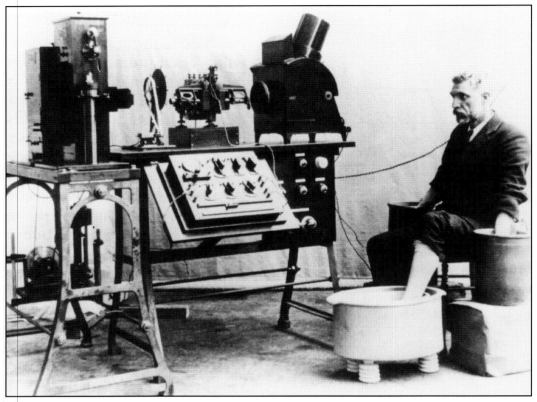

A patient is hooked up to an early EKG machine in 1908.

and what could be done to treat heart problems. The invention and improvement of medical devices like microscopes and stethoscopes also helped.

Surgery for different body parts became more common. Surgical procedures were practiced and improved and as time passed, patients were more likely to survive after serious surgeries. The heart was considered too delicate to treat directly with surgical treatment until the last one hundred years.

HEART SURGERY

During World War II (1939 to 1945), military doctors were faced with the task of treating soldiers with heart injuries. Many soldiers had pieces of metal or bullets stuck in their hearts. One of the first doctors to attempt heart surgery was Dwight Harken, an American military doctor. He tried heart surgery on animals first. Dr. Harken found that he could make a small hole in the heart and reach in with his finger to remove objects that did not belong in

Etienne-Louis Fallot was a French doctor who discovered the reason why some babies develop blue skin. The medical condition Tetralogy of Fallot was named after him.

the heart. Soon he felt ready to try his technique on humans. He was able to remove pieces of metal and bullets from soldiers' hearts. Luckily, all of his patients lived. But the technique was not useful for other types of heart disease that were not caused by injury. For example, serious heart defects required opening the heart.

But doctors were afraid to open up a person's heart for major surgery, because the patient would bleed to death. During the

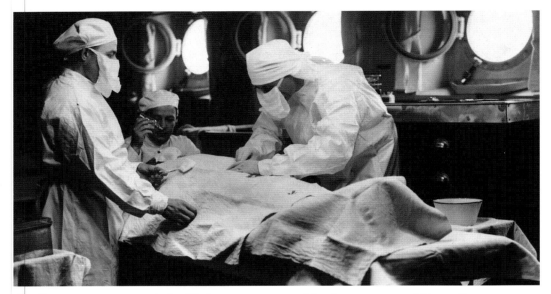

Wartime surgeons operated with few resources and in dangerous conditions. However, their contributions to medical research have helped to develop useful technologies and procedures.

late 1940s, a Canadian doctor named Bill Bigelow tried to figure out a way to help a patient through major surgery. He knew that when bears hibernated in winter, their hearts beat much more slowly and their bodies needed less oxygen. Dr. Bigelow thought that it might be possible to put human patients in something like a state of hibernation by cooling them down. Then a doctor could operate on the heart, and then warm them up again after the surgery was finished.

In 1952, Dr. Walton Lillehei and Dr. John Lewis used this theory to operate on a five-year-old girl who had patent ductus arteriosus. They cooled her body down, which slowed her heart. They knew they would only have about ten minutes to fix her heart before the lack of oxygen would affect her brain.

The surgery worked. They were able to repair the problem and warm the girl back to her normal body temperature. This type of surgery, however, could not work for all heart defects because surgeons had only a few minutes to work on the heart. If the heart defects were very serious or extensive, a few minutes would not be enough time to operate. Another problem with these early forms of open-heart surgery was that the heart was still beating and moving during the operation. Although this was important to keep the patient alive, it made it very difficult for a surgeon to operate on the heart itself.

The next major development in heart surgery was the invention of the heart-lung machine. In 1958, doctors

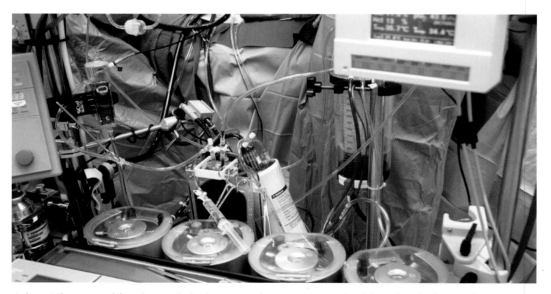

A heart-lung machine is used during open-heart surgery. Besides circulating and oxygenating blood, the machine can also deliver medication, and control blood levels and temperature.

perfected a machine that would temporarily do the work of the heart and lungs while doctors fixed the heart. The heart-lung machine draws blood out of the body through a tube, cleans it, adds fresh oxygen, and pumps it back into the body. This gave doctors much more time to fix the heart. Doctors also invented a medication to use on the patient during surgery that temporarily stopped the heart from beating. This medication, along with the heart-lung machine, was a very important improvement for heart surgeons and their patients.

An important role which these advances played (in addition to saving lives) was allowing doctors to see diseased hearts up close for the first time. When Dr. Harken and Dr. Bigelow were performing some of the first heart surgeries, they often found other problems within the heart that they did not expect. Before open-heart surgeries were performed, doctors had only been able to make educated guesses about heart problems. They could now see the problems up close.

New technologies also helped. Chemical tests and other devices were created to help observe the heart and its functions. New medications such as antibiotics helped people recover after heart surgery.

TRANSPLANTS

In the 1960s doctors attempted heart transplants. These surgeries were performed on people whose hearts could not be repaired. A healthy donor heart from a person who had just died was surgically placed into the chest of someone who had his or her diseased heart removed. These were complicated surgeries that took a lot of time. At first, many patients who had transplants died of infections or their bodies rejected the new heart.

During the 1970s doctors found ways to prevent the body from rejecting transplanted

In 1968, Dr. Norman Shumway and a team of surgeons performed the United States' first successful human heart transplant.

hearts. Drugs were developed to keep the body from reacting to the donor heart. Other medications and techniques helped people live longer after a transplant surgery. By using certain

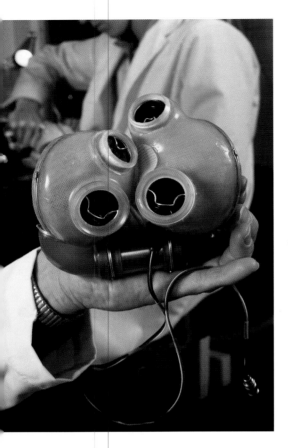

In the early 1980s, an artificial heart made of aluminum and plastic was implanted in a patient who was able to survive with it for more than 100 days. Today, scientists are looking for new ways to design a permanent artificial heart.

drugs, people who underwent transplants could live longer. Like all organ transplants, heart transplants are very serious operations. But as time passed, these surgeries became more common. Today they are still used and are often successful.

THE FUTURE

Every day scientists learn something new about heart disease. Many medicines have been developed to treat heart conditions. For many heart problems, surgery is only used as a last resort. Plus all the knowledge that doctors have gained through the years has helped with prevention. People now know what they can do to keep their hearts healthy.

In 2001, doctors began testing the use of entirely manmade artificial hearts. Artificial hearts could help hundreds of thousands of people who are waiting for new hearts. But more testing must be done before artificial hearts are used regularly.

Researchers around the world continue to find ways to prevent, diagnose, and treat heart disease.

Researchers are also working with heart cells that they made with real human tissue. Someday they may be able to transplant non-artificial hearts created in the laboratory. These hearts would be made up of real human tissue. Although it will be many years before a heart like this can be tested in humans, there is hope for the millions of people with heart disease.

4

LIVING WITH HEART DISEASE

PREVENTION

Sometimes heart disease can be prevented. Learning about things such as **heredity** and risk factors can help a person prevent heart disease.

Family History and Risk Factors

Heart disease can be genetic. This means that if a member of a person's family has had heart disease, other people in the family are more likely to develop heart disease as well. It does not mean that a person will definitely develop heart disease just because a relative has it. A person cannot control genetics. He or she cannot help having family members with heart disease. But when a person has a family history of heart disease, it is important to try to control the risk factors. Risk factors are things that make it more likely that a person will

A healthy diet consists of appropriate servings of food groups illustrated in this food group pyramid. The groups include (from the top) fats, oils, and sweets; meat, poultry, fish, and eggs; milk and cheese; vegetables; fruits; and bread, cereal, rice, and pasta.

Fatty foods and foods that have been fried usually have a lot of cholesterol. Too much of these foods can lead to plaque buildup in the arteries.

develop heart disease. For example, smoking cigarettes is a risk factor for heart disease. Obesity (being very overweight) is another risk factor.

Diet and Exercise

The foods you eat have an effect on the health of your heart. A diet with a lot of fat increases the risk of heart disease. Foods high in fat are also often high in **cholesterol**. Cholesterol is a fatty substance found in food, which can build up in arteries as plaque. Eating a nutritious diet that is low in fat and cholesterol can help prevent heart disease.

Being overweight is a risk factor because it puts extra strain on the heart. The heavier a person is, the harder the heart has to work to pump blood through the body. But a person should check with his or her doctor to determine what a healthy weight is. (It is important to remember that each person is different, so not everybody needs to weigh the same amount.) Eating a healthful diet can help a person maintain his or her appropriate weight.

Exercise helps prevent weight gain and keeps the heart fit. When people engage in physical activity, the heart pumps a little faster and a little harder. When done in moderation (not too much and not too little) this is good exercise for the heart muscle. A doctor or other health professional can help determine how much and what type of exercise is right for each person.

Regular physical activity can help a person maintain his or her weight, strengthen muscles, and exercise the heart. However, people with heart conditions should ask their doctors about the right amount and type of exercise.

Smoking

Studies have shown that smoking cigarettes and other tobacco products (pipes, cigars) is very bad for your health. It can cause cancer in the lungs, throat, and mouth. It can also lead to heart disease. One of the best ways to prevent heart disease is not to smoke. People who do smoke should consider quitting.

Stress

We all experience stress in our lives. Stress can make a person feel very anxious, worried, or upset. Stress can be a positive thing. It can help us recognize things that are not going well so we can make good changes in our lives. However, too much stress can lead to high blood pressure, which can lead to other kinds of health problems. These may include heart attack, stroke, and congestive heart failure. To reduce stress, many people may need to change what they do, or learn not to become as anxious or worried. If they work very long hours, they might try to reduce their workload. Many people also find relaxing hobbies that help to reduce stress. These may include woodworking, quilting, sewing, or other craft projects. Others practice meditation or yoga. These are relaxing forms of sitting or movement that calm a person and improve blood pressure.

A mother and daughter practice yoga. Many people do yoga to reduce stress while also stretching and strengthening their muscles.

Coping with Heart Disease

It is not always possible to prevent heart disease. Some people are born with the disease. Others do not realize they need to change their lifestyle until they develop the disease. Whatever the case may be, there is still hope for people with heart disease. Besides maintaining an overall healthy lifestyle, there are many things that people can do to cope with heart disease.

Heart Monitoring

Certain kinds of heart disease require monitoring of the heart at home. If someone has an arrhythmia, he or she might need to take his or her pulse every day to make sure the heart rate is within normal limits. If someone has high blood pressure, he or she might check blood pressure readings every day. Keeping a log of heart rate and blood pressure can help doctors learn when the problem is at its worse, which can help them choose the right treatment.

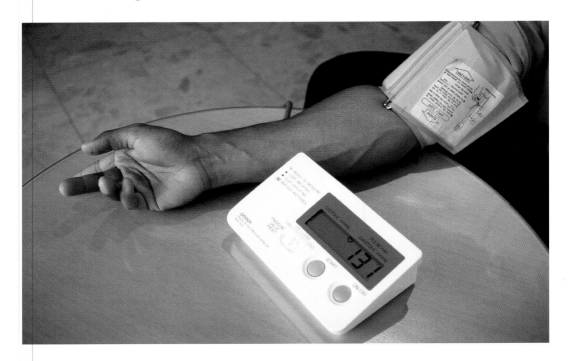

A person can easily monitor his or her blood pressure with an electronic or digital sphygmomanometer. By simply pushing a button, the battery-operated device pumps air into the cuff, releases the air, measures the blood pressure, and displays the results on a small screen.

Medication

Often, people with heart disease take medication to help control their symptoms. For example, high blood pressure can often be treated with changes in diet, increased exercise, quitting smoking, and better stress management. Some people need medication to help bring blood pressure to a healthy level. Some people only need to take medication until the changes in diet, exercise, and stress improve their blood pressure. But most need to take medication for the rest of their lives.

It is important for people with heart disease to take their medication exactly as the doctor has prescribed. Missing doses, taking medication at the wrong time, or taking too much

Barking for Lower Blood Pressure

Research has shown that having a pet may reduce high blood pressure. In one study, people with high blood pressure were given a pet, usually a dog or a cat. After six months, these people were better able to handle stressful situations, and their blood pressure was not as high during those stressful times. Many believe that the pets have a calming effect. The companionship of a pet can help a person relax, which in turn lowers blood pressure. (It is important to remember, however, that doctors do not think that a person should get a pet *instead* of seeking proper medical treatment for hypertension.)

Pets can be beneficial to a person's emotional and physical well being.

Many people who take several pills each day use special pill dispensers. These containers help a person remember which pills to take at what time, or on what day.

medication can be dangerous. People who must take several kinds of medications should write down a schedule to make sure each one is taken at the correct dose, and at the right time.

Recovering from Surgery

If someone has had heart surgery, he or she must see a doctor regularly afterward. Doctors want to make sure that the heart is working properly. The person also might need to take antibiotics before having dental work or having other surgery. This is to prevent infections in heart tissue.

Hospitals and health centers across the country offer cardiac rehabilitation programs for people who have heart conditions or people who have had heart surgery. At these programs, people can safely exercise under the watchful eyes of healthcare professionals. This is especially important for heart patients who should not overwork their hearts while exercising. The programs can also serve as support systems, bringing together people with shared problems and experiences. Some heart patients attend these exercise sessions many times a week. Many take part in the cardiac rehabilitation programs for the rest of their lives.

Support

One of the most important things a person with heart disease can do is to talk with others. People with heart disease should always talk to their doctors and follow their advice. But there are also other people who can help. Millions of people around

Heart patients exercise together as part of a cardiac rehabilitation program.

the country have heart disease. Together with their families and with healthcare professionals, they have formed support groups. These support groups offer counseling and other services to help patients and their families. Some people find it easier to cope with heart disease when they can talk with other people who know what they are going through.

There are many treatments for heart disease and researchers continue to find more ways to help people. By understanding the disease, people with heart disease can still live life to the fullest. Knowledge is the key to coping with heart disease.

GLOSSARY

abdomen—The part of the body that lies between the chest and the hips.

angioplasty—A surgical procedure designed to open blocked arteries.

aorta—The largest artery in the human body.

arrhythmia—An irregular (abnormal) heart rate.

arteries—Blood vessels that carry blood away from the heart.

atrium—One of the two upper chambers of the heart. ("Atria" is used when talking about more than one atrium.)

bradycardia—A type of arrhythmia in which the heart beats too slowly.

chambers—Enclosed spaces inside the body or an organ. The heart has four chambers.

cholesterol—A fatty substance that can build up in arteries. The body makes some of its own cholesterol, but cholesterol can also be found in food.

diagnose—To determine what is making a person sick.

dissect—To examine something by separating it into pieces.

electrocardiogram—A medical test that measures electrical heart activity; also known as an EKG.

faint—To pass out or lose consciousness. People may faint when they are sick.

heredity—The passing on of traits from parents to their children.

hypertension—High blood pressure.

myocardium—A special type of muscle tissue found in the heart.

nutritious—To be a useful to and healthy for the body.

pacemaker—A device inserted into the body to help regulate heartbeats.

plaque—A substance that builds up and covers or blocks something.

pericardium—The outer lining of the heart. It protects the heart and helps to hold it in place.

prematurely—Early.

rehabilitation—The process of making something healthy or useful again.

septum—A wall of muscle that divides the heart into right and left sides.

sinoatrial node—The heart's command center, located in the upper right region of the heart. It delivers an electrical impulse to the heart muscle, which makes the heart beat.

sphygmomanometer—A device used to measure blood pressure.

stent—A wire mesh tube that holds an artery open so blood can flow freely through it.

stress—Conditions or situations that can cause feelings of anxiety or worry.

tachycardia—A type of arrhythmia in which the heart beats too quickly.

valves—One-way openings through which blood can flow forward, but not backward.

veins—Blood vessels that bring blood from the body to the heart.

ventricles—The two lower chambers of the heart.

venules—Tiny veins.

FIND OUT MORE

The American Heart Association
7272 Greenville Avenue
Dallas, TX 75231
1-800-AHA-USA-1 (1-800-242-8721)
www.americanheart.org

The American Heart Association provides helpful information about heart health, heart disease, and stroke. You can also find information about heart-related organizations and activities near you.

Books

American Heart Association. *American Heart Association Kids' Cookbook*. New York: Random Hosue/Times Books, 1993.

Gray, Shirley W. *Exercising for Good Health*. Chanhassen, MN: Child's World, 2004.

Gregson, Susan R. *Heart Disease*. Mankato, MN: LifeMatters, 2001.

LeVert, Suzanne. *The Heart*. New York: Benchmark Books, 2002.

Mayo Clinic Health Information. *8 Ways to Lower Your Risk of a Heart Attack or Stroke*. Broomall, PA: Mason Crest Publishers, 2002.

Sheps, Sheldon G. *Mayo Clinic on High Blood Pressure*. Broomall, PA: Mason Crest Publishers, 2002.

Simon, Seymour. *The Heart: Our Circulatory System*. New York: Morrow Junior Books, 1996.

Web Sites

Congenital Heart Information Network
http://www.tchin.org

HeartCenterOnline
http://www.heartcenteronline.com

The Heart and the Circulatory System
http://www.accessexcellence.org/AE/AEC/CC/
heart_background.html

Heart and Stroke Foundation of Canada
http://ww1.heartandstroke.ca

Heart Diseases (U.S. National Library of Medicine and the
National Institutes of Health)
http://www.nlm.nih.gov/medlineplus/heartdiseases.html

KidsHealth For Kids: All About the Heart
http://kidshealth.org/kid/body/heart_noSW.html

Kids Corner—Let's Learn About Your Heart
(Minneapolis Heart Institute Foundation)
http://www.mplsheartfoundation.org/kids

The Mended Hearts, Inc.
http://www.mendedhearts.org

National Heart, Lung, and Blood Institute (NHLBI)
http://www.nhlbi.nih.gov

NOVA Online: Electric Heart
http://www.pbs.org/wgbh/nova/eheart

Texas Heart Institute
http://www.texasheartinstitute.org

INDEX

Page numbers for illustrations are in **boldface**

history, 36–45, **37**, **38**, **39**, **40**, **43**, **44**
hospital, 8, 25
hypertension, 24, 29–31, **29**, 34
    See also blood pressure

Lewis, John, 40
Lillehei, Walton, 40
lungs, 6, 7, 16, 17, 19, 20, 22, 23, 24, 34

medication, 19, 26, 32, 43, 44, 53–54, **54**
meditation, 50, 51, **51**
muscle, 10, 31, 32
myocardial infarction (MI), *See* heart attack.
myocardium, 10, 24–25, 31, 33, 49

nitroglycerin, 26
nutrition, 8, 47, **47**, 48

obesity, 48
oxygen, 9, 15, 16, 17, 19, 22, 23, 24–25, 31,
    41, 42

pacemaker, 32, 33, **33**
pain, 8, 25
Patent Ductus Arteriosus (PDA), 19, 40
pericardium, 10
pets, 53, **53**
physicians, 8, 25, 26, 35, 36, 37, 38, 39, **39**,
    48–49, 55
    visits, 6, 7, 9
plaque, 9, 24–25, **25**, 27, 29, 48
pulse, 18

research, 44–45, **44**, **45**
risk factors, 46, 48

septal defects, 19–20
    AV, 20
septum, 12, 19–20
sinoatrial node, 11
skin, 6
    blue, 22, **22**

smoking, 6, 32, 50
sphygmomanometer, 29, **29**, 52, **52**
statistics, 18, 24, 31, 33, 35, 55
stent, 27
stethoscope, **18**, 29, **29**, 38
stress, 9, 32, 50–51, **51**, 52, 53
stroke, 31, 37, **37**
support, 54, 55
surgery, 38, 39, 40, **40**
    recovery, 54–55, **56**

tachycardia, 31, 32
technology, 42, 44, 45, **44**, **45**
Transposition of the Great Arteries, 23–24
treatment, 32, 36–38, 46–55

valves, 12, 13, **13**, 33, 35
veins, 15, 27, 28, **28**, 34
vena cava
    lower, 16, **16**
    upper, 16, **16**
ventricles, 12, 13, **13**, 16–17, 20, 22
venules, 15

weight, 48–49
World War II, 39

yoga, 50–51, **51**

63

ABOUT THE AUTHOR

Johannah Haney is a writer living in Boston, Massachusetts. She has written several textbooks and articles for magazines. Ms. Haney lives with her two cats, who help keep her blood pressure low.